Lockhart

by Iain Gray

WRITING *to* REMEMBER

79 Main Street, Newtongrange,
Midlothian EH22 4NA
Tel: 0131 344 0414
E-mail: info@lang-syne.co.uk
www.langsyneshop.co.uk

Design by Dorothy Meikle
Printed by Blissetts
© Lang Syne Publishers Ltd 2024

All rights reserved. No part of this publication may be reproduced, stored or introduced into a retrieval system, or transmitted in any form or by any means (electronic, mechanical, photocopying, recording or otherwise) without the prior written permission of Lang Syne Publishers Ltd.

ISBN 978-1-85217-763-8

Lockhart

MOTTO:
I open closed hearts

CREST:
A boar's head

TERRITORIES:
Ayrshire, Lanarkshire

NAME variations include:
Locard
Lockard
Lockheart

Chapter one:

The origins of the clan system

by Rennie McOwan

The original Scottish clans of the Highlands and the great families of the Lowlands and Borders were gatherings of families, relatives, allies and neighbours for mutual protection against rivals or invaders.

Scotland experienced invasion from the Vikings, the Romans and English armies from the south. The Norman invasion of what is now England also had an influence on land-holding in Scotland. Some of these invaders stayed on and in time became 'Scottish'.

The word clan derives from the Gaelic language term 'clann', meaning children, and it was first used many centuries ago as communities were formed around tribal lands in glens and mountain fastnesses.

The format of clans changed over the centuries, but at its best the chief and his family held the land on behalf of all, like trustees, and the ordinary clansmen and women believed they had a blood relationship with the founder of their clan.

There were two way duties and obligations. An inadequate chief could be deposed and replaced by someone of greater ability.

Clan people had an immense pride in race. Their relationship with the chief was like adult children to a father and they had a real dignity.

The concept of clanship is very old and a more feudal notion of authority gradually crept in.

Pictland, for instance, was divided into seven principalities ruled by feudal leaders who were the strongest and most charismatic leaders of their particular groups.

By the sixth century the 'British' kingdoms of Strathclyde, Lothian and Celtic Dalriada (Argyll) had emerged and Scotland, as one nation, began to take shape in the time of King Kenneth MacAlpin.

Some chiefs claimed descent from ancient kings which may not have been accurate in every case.

By the twelfth and thirteenth centuries the clans and families were more strongly brought under the central control of Scottish monarchs.

Lands were awarded and administered more and more under royal favour, yet the power of the area clan chiefs was still very great.

The long wars to ensure Scotland's

independence against the expansionist ideas of English monarchs extended the influence of some clans and reduced the lands of others.

Those who supported Scotland's greatest king, Robert the Bruce, were awarded the territories of the families who had opposed his claim to the Scottish throne.

In the Scottish Borders country – the notorious Debatable Lands – the great families built up a ferocious reputation for providing warlike men accustomed to raiding into England and occasionally fighting one another.

Chiefs had the power to dispense justice and to confiscate lands and clan warfare produced a society where martial virtues – courage, hardiness, tenacity – were greatly admired.

Gradually the relationship between the clans and the Crown became strained as Scottish monarchs became more orientated to life in the Lowlands and, on occasion, towards England.

The Highland clans spoke a different language, Gaelic, whereas the language of Lowland Scotland and the court was Scots and in more modern times, English.

Highlanders dressed differently, had different

customs, and their wild mountain land sometimes seemed almost foreign to people living in the Lowlands.

It must be emphasised that Gaelic culture was very rich and story-telling, poetry, piping, the clarsach (harp) and other music all flourished and were greatly respected.

Highland culture was different from other parts of Scotland but it was not inferior or less sophisticated.

Central Government, whether in London or Edinburgh, sometimes saw the Gaelic clans as a challenge to their authority and some sent expeditions into the Highlands and west to crush the power of the Lords of the Isles.

Nevertheless, when the eighteenth century Jacobite Risings came along the cause of the Stuarts was mainly supported by Highland clans.

The word Jacobite comes from the Latin for James – Jacobus. The Jacobites wanted to restore the exiled Stuarts to the throne of Britain.

The monarchies of Scotland and England became one in 1603 when King James VI of Scotland (1st of England) gained the English throne after Queen Elizabeth died.

The Union of Parliaments of Scotland and England, the Treaty of Union, took place in 1707.

Some Highland clans, of course, and Lowland families opposed the Jacobites and supported the incoming Hanoverians.

After the Jacobite cause finally went down at Culloden in 1746 a kind of ethnic cleansing took place. The power of the chiefs was curtailed. Tartan and the pipes were banned in law.

Many emigrated, some because they wanted to, some because they were evicted by force. In addition, many Highlanders left for the cities of the south to seek work.

Many of the clan lands became home to sheep and deer shooting estates.

But the warlike traditions of the clans and the great Lowland and Border families lived on, with their descendants fighting bravely for freedom in two world wars.

Remember the men from whence you came, says the Gaelic proverb, and to that could be added the role of many heroic women.

The spirit of the clan, of having roots, whether Highland or Lowland, means much to thousands of people.

Meanwhile, many families proudly boast the heraldic device known as a Coat of Arms,.

The central motif of the Coat of Arms would originally have been what was sometimes borne on the shield of a warrior to distinguish himself from others on the battlefield.

Clan warfare produced a society where courage and tenacity were greatly admired

Chapter two:

Bravehearts

A name that features prominently in Scotland's historical record since the late eleventh century, 'Lockhart' has two possible points of origin.

Also found from early times in forms that include 'Locard', 'Lockard' and 'Lockheart', a Scottish source is from a German personal name containing the element 'loc', meaning 'lock', while 'hart' indicates 'hard' – and therefore signifying someone renowned for strength, steadfastness and bravery.

According to Lockhart family tradition, their forebears were forced to quit their original territory in the north of England in the late eleventh century.

This was in the aftermath of a vicious purge launched against them and fellow Anglo-Saxon aristocrats and Danish settlers by William the Conqueror, victor of the battle of Hastings in 1066.

Following his defeat of King Harold II, the last Anglo-Saxon king, William was declared king and the complete subjugation of his Anglo-Saxon subjects followed, with those Normans who had fought on his behalf rewarded with the lands of Anglo-Saxons.

But trouble brewed for William in the north of his new realm, where Anglo-Danish rebellions had been stirred by Edgar Atheling, claimant to what had been the kingdom of Wessex.

In what is known as The Harrying of the North, William's response was brutal – laying waste from 1069 to 1070 to the northern shires, including the city of York and replacing native aristocracy, such as those who would come to bear the Lockhart name in Scotland, with Normans deemed to be more loyal.

In 1071, King Malcolm III of Scotland married Margaret, a sister of Edgar Atheling and therefore had an affinity with the dispossessed northerners – welcoming them to settle in his realm.

The Lockharts, possibly originally settled in Penrith, in the Eden Valley area of present-day Cumbria, did not initially have to travel far over the border to settle in Scotland – with the Annandale town of Lockerbie reputed to have been named after them.

Sir Symon Locard, 2nd of Lee, is recorded in 1323 as holding the lands of Lee and Cartland, in present-day South Lanarkshire, while in Ayrshire his grandfather – also named Symon – founded the village of Stevenston and one of his uncles the village of Symons Town, better known today as Symington.

Lanarkshire and Ayrshire came to be recognised as the main territories of the Lockharts, with Lee Castle, near Lanark, the seat of the Chief of Clan Lockhart.

Steadfast in their support for the cause of Scotland's freedom during the Wars of Independence with England, the Lockharts gained fame for their role in a mission entrusted to them and other members of their warrior class in the wake of the death of the great warrior king Robert the Bruce.

Victor of the battle of Bannockburn in 1314 – in the aftermath of which Sir Symon of Locard of Lee was knighted in recognition of having fought at his side – Bruce died on June 7, 1329 at his manor house of Cardross, near Dumbarton.

But before being embalmed and interred with great pomp and ceremony at Dunfermline Abbey, his sternum was sawn open and his heart extracted.

It had long been his wish to undertake a crusade to the Holy Land and, having failed in this, his final instruction was that his heart be carried instead to be placed before the Holy Sepulchre in Jerusalem, and then returned to Scotland to be buried in Melrose Abbey.

Accordingly, his loyal follower Sir James

Douglas placed the embalmed heart in a casket, placing it on a chain around his neck and entrusting the key to Sir Symon Locard of Lee.

They then left Scottish shores along with others faithful to Bruce's wishes who included the brothers Sir Robert Logan and Sir Walter Logan, Sir William Keith and the brothers Sir William Sinclair of Roslin and Sir John Sinclair.

But a European crusade to the Holy Land had never materialised, and Sir James Douglas and his band instead sailed for Spain where King Alfonso XI of Castile was set to mount a campaign against the Moorish kingdom of Granada.

The battle-hardened Scots were gratefully welcomed and, in August of 1330 formed part of Alfonso's Christian army that was besieging the castle of Teba.

In a vicious battle against the foe, Sir James and his compatriots were surrounded and most of them killed – including Douglas and the Logan brothers – but not before Douglas had hurled the precious casket before him, shouting: "Lead on brave heart, I'll follow thee" or, as other accounts state: "Go first as thou hast always done."

The casket and Sir Douglas's body were

recovered from the carnage of the battlefield by Sir Symon Locard and the few Scots who had survived and returned to Scotland – where, in accordance with Bruce's wishes, his heart was buried in Melrose Abbey.

But Bruce's heart was not destined to rest in peace.

Archaeologists excavating the grounds of the by-then ruined abbey in 1921 discovered a casket buried there, and then reburied it in an unmarked spot.

In 1996, an archaeological team from Historic Scotland (now Historic Environment Scotland) excavated a lead container while working on the floor of the abbey's chapter house.

A small hole was carefully drilled in the container and a fibre-optic probe inserted to examine what was inside. The casket was then opened to reveal another, smaller, lead container, with an inscribed copper plaque stating:

"The enclosed leaden casket containing a heart was found beneath Chapter House floor, March 1921, by His Majesty's Office of Works."

The casket was found to contain human tissue and Richard Welander, one of the experts who examined it, stated that although it was not possible to prove with certainty that the casket contained the remains of Bruce's heart, it was reasonable to assume so.

The casket was reburied in a private ceremony at the abbey on June 22, 1998 and, in a more public ceremony held on June 24, the anniversary of the battle of Bannockburn, Donald Dewar, Secretary of State for Scotland, unveiled a sandstone marker with the inscription by the fourteenth century poet John Barbour, author of the epic The Bruce:

A Noble Hart May Have Nane
Ease Gif Freedom Failye
(A noble heart can know no ease without freedom)

Mr Dewar, who described the ceremony as one of great significance and symbolism for the people of Scotland, added: "There is a strong and proper presumption that this is the heart, but in a sense it does not matter.

"The casket and the heart are symbols of the man".

Sir Symon Locard's role in the affair of Bruce's heart is proudly commemorated through the central motif of Clan Lockhart's Coat of Arms featuring a heart with a fetterlock, and the motto 'I open closed hearts.'

The clan crest, meanwhile, different from the central motif, features a boar's head – aptly symbolic of strength and bravery.

In contemporary times, the castellated mansion of Lee Castle in Auchenglen, near Lanark and also known as The Lee, has passed into private ownership – but the present Chief of Clan Lockhart still manages a substantial landholding at nearby Carnwath.

Also, in addition to their own proud heritage and traditions, because of a close association for centuries with Clan Douglas, in July of 2012 the Lockharts were formally recognised as an 'allied family' of the Douglases.

Chapter three:

Dynastic heritage

It was not only with Bruce's heart that Sir Symon Locard returned to Scotland, but also a precious amulet reputed to have miraculous healing powers.

While fighting the Moors, he had captured one of their army's amirs, or lords and, in keeping with the custom of relating to wealthy prisoners, he held him to ransom.

Anxious for his safe return, the distraught amir's mother settled the ransom with not only gold and jewellery but also a mysterious stone that, she assured Sir Symon, acted as a proven remedy for a host of ailments including 'bleeding a fever, the bite of a mad dog and sickness in horses and cattle.'

Dark red in colour and triangular in shape, the amulet's properties could be activated through dipping it in water.

Sir Symon's descendants later had the amulet set in a silver coin, now known to date from the reign of England's King Edward IV (1461-1470), and in the late eighteenth century, placed in a gold snuffbox gifted in 1789 by Empress Maria Theresa of Austria to James Lockhart of Lee and Carnwath.

Known as the Lee Penny, knowledge of the stone's healing powers became widespread and it was loaned on occasion to work its magic.

This includes during the reign from 1625 to 1649 of King Charles I when it was loaned to the citizens of Newcastle to protect against an outbreak of plague.

So precious was the Lee Penny considered that a substantial sum of money had to be pledged by the citizens as guarantee of its safe return.

Still in the family's proud possession to this day, the Lee Penny was also the inspiration for Sir Walter Scott's 1825 novel *The Talisman*.

In the centuries following the gifting of the amulet to Sir Symon Locard, his descendants continued at the forefront of pivotal events in Scotland's turbulent history and often at great cost.

A son of the family of the Lockharts of Lee, Sir Alan Lockhart was among the many Scots slain in the disastrous battle of Pinkie, fought on September 10, 1547, near Musselburgh, in East Lothian, when a 25,000-strong English army under the Duke of

Somerset decisively defeated a 35,000-strong Scots army under the Earl of Arran.

Also known as the battle of Pinkie Cleugh, it was fought during the 'Rough Wooing', an attempt by England's dynastically ambitious Henry VIII to force upon the Scots agreement for the future marriage of his infant son Edward to the infant Mary, Queen of Scots.

Despite their superior numbers, what led to the defeat of the Scots in what became known as 'Black Saturday' was that Somerset was backed by a fleet of naval guns at the mouth of the River Esk, and the early loss in the battle of the Scots cavalry after it launched a premature and wild charge on the massed and disciplined English ranks.

During the civil wars known as the Wars of the Three Kingdoms that raged in the seventeenth century between Royalists and Parliamentarians, Sir James Lockhart was the courtier, politician and judge who commanded a Royalist regiment under the Marquis of Hamilton at the battle of Preston in 1648.

He died in 1674 while his son Sir William Lockhart, born in 1621, having initially supported the Royalist cause, was the soldier and diplomat who, after reconciling himself to the Parliamentarian Oliver Cromwell, married one of his nieces.

Having served in a number of diplomatic posts after Scotland was 'inaugurated' into the English Commonwealth, he died in 1675.

With the Lockharts of Lee staunch Jacobites – those who sought the deposition of the House of Hanover and the restoration to the throne of the Royal House of Stuart – Sir George Lockhart of Lee, born in 1673, was the politician and writer who served as Principal Envoy to James Francis Edward Stuart, 'the Old Pretender', after the abortive Jacobite Rising of 1715.

Author of the *Lockhart Papers*, an invaluable source on Jacobite history, he died in 1731, while his grandson George Lockhart served as personal aide-de-camp to Charles Edward Stuart, the 'Young Pretender,' during the equally ill-fated '45 Rising – accompanying him into exile following defeat at the battle of Culloden in 1746.

His younger brother James Lockhart of Lee and Carnwath, also titled Count Lockhart-Wishart of the Holy Roman Empire, born in 1727, was the distinguished military commander who enlisted in the Austrian army to fight under the banner of Empress

Maria Theresa during the War of the Austrian Succession.

Gaining high rank and honours, it was he who received the gift from the Empress of the gold snuffbox that now holds the Lee Penny; he died in 1790.

In addition to the celebrated Lockharts of Lee, another noted dynasty is the 'Bruce Lockharts' – a distinguished family of schoolmasters, spies, diplomats, authors and sportsmen.

Born in 1889 in the village of Beith, in one of the Lockhart homelands of Ayrshire, John Harold 'J.H.' Bruce Lockhart was the schoolmaster, cricketer and rugby player who served for a time as a housemaster at Rugby School and as the first headmaster of Spier's School, Beith.

Representing Scotland as a rugby fly half and also as a cricketer, he died in 1956, while his sons Rab, born in 1916, and Logie, born in 1921, also represented their nation on the rugby pitch.

He was also a brother of the diplomat, spy and author Sir Robert Hamilton Bruce Lockhart, born in 1887. As an MI6 operative in Moscow, he was caught in a 'sting' operation orchestrated by Bolshevik spymasters as he attempted, along with fellow spy

Sidney Reilly, to sabotage the revolution and sentenced to death *in abstentia*.

Author in 1932 of the best-selling *Memoirs of a British Agent*, he worked for a time as editor of the *Londoner's Diary* column for the *Evening Standard* newspaper and, during the Second World War, as director-general of the Political Warfare Executive (PWE).

He died in 1970, while he was the father of the author Robin Bruce Lockhart, born in 1920 and who died in 2008, and whose 1967 book *Ace of Spies*, based on Sidney Reilly and also referencing his own father, was adapted for television in 1983 as *Reilly: Ace of Spies*.

The actor Ian Charleson took on the role of his father, while Sam Neill played Reilly.

Another of the sons of John Harold 'J.H.' Bruce Lockhart, James Macgregor Bruce Lockhart was the schoolmaster, diplomat, soldier and intelligence officer born in Rugby in 1914.

A rugby player, in common with other members of his family, he served in the Secret Intelligence Service (SIS), or MI6, during the Second World War and later as First Secretary at the British Embassy in Washington DC.

He died in 1995, while his son James Robert Bruce Lockhart, born in 1941 and who died in 2018, also worked for MI6, under 'cover' of working for the Foreign Office.

He was the father of the actor and director Dugald Bruce Lockhart, born in Fiji in 1968.

Having worked as an actor with the National Theatre Company and Royal Shakespeare Company, he has been an associate director since 1998 of the all-male theatre company Propeller, while at the Edinburgh Festival in 2013 he was nominated best actor by *The Stage* for his role of then Conservative Prime Minister David Cameron in the play *The Three Lions*.

Not related to the Bruce Lockharts, but no less notable, Sir James Haldane Stewart Lockhart was the Scottish colonial official in Hong Kong and China recognised today as a pioneering Sinologist – a scholar of Chinese language and culture – and who made a number of important translations.

Born in 1858 in Ardsheal, Argyllshire and entering the Colonial Service in 1878 after failing in an attempt to enter the civil service in India – to the ultimate gain of Sinology – he died in 1937.

Chapter four:

On the world stage

From the stage and sport to music, art and literature, bearers of the Lockhart name have gained international fame and acclaim.

One of a dynasty of stage, television and film actors, Kathleen Arthur was the British-American actress better known by her married name **Kathleen Lockhart**.

Born in 1894 in Southsea, Hampshire, she appeared on stage in Britain before immigrating to the United States and going on to appear in more than 300 films including, along with her second husband **Gene Lockhart** and her then 13-year-old daughter June, as Mrs Bob Cratchit in the 1938 *A Christmas Carol*.

The recipient of a star on the Hollywood Walk of Fame, she died in 1978 while her husband Gene Lockhart was the Canadian-American actor, playwright, singer and lyricist born in 1891 in London, Ontario.

Making his stage debut when aged only six, he wrote the musical *The Pierrot Players*, including its popular song *The World is Waiting for the Sunrise* – since covered by a range of artists including Duke Ellington, Willie Nelson and the Beatles.

Other stage work included the 1949 production of Death of a Salesman, while film credits – in addition to *A Christmas Carol* as Bob Cratchit – include the 1938 *Algiers*, which won him an Academy Award nomination for Best Supporting Actor.

The recipient of two stars on the Hollywood Walk of Fame – for motion pictures and television work – he died in 1957.

He and his wife Kathleen were the parents of the award-winning American actress **June Lockhart**, who made her film debut in 1938 along with her parents in *A Christmas Carol*.

Born in 1925 and having worked mainly in television, she is best known for her Emmy-Award winning roles throughout the 1950s and 1960s in popular series including *Lassie* and *Lost in Space*.

Other television credits include the Westerns *Wagon Train*, *Gunsmoke* and *Rawhide*, while big screen credits include the 1941 *Sergeant York*, the 1944 *Meet Me in St Louis* and, from 1946, *She-Wolf of London*.

In common with her father she is the recipient of two stars on the Hollywood Walk of Fame, for motion pictures and television, while she is also the mother of the actress **Anne Lockhart**.

Born Anne Kathleen Maloney – with 'Maloney' the surname of her mother's first husband – in New York City in 1953, she is best known for her role of Lieutenant Sheba in the original *Battlefield Galactica* television series.

Born in 1934 in Nassau, Bahamas, the youngest of eight children, Bert McClossy Cooper was the acclaimed Bahamian-American actor of stage and screen better known as **Calvin Lockhart**.

Immigrating to the United States when aged 18, he studied engineering and then ran a carpentry business in New York before realising his acting ambition by making his Broadway debut in 1960 in *The Cool World*.

Working in Britain for a time, his career thrived as he landed roles in a number of films including the 1968 *A Dandy in Aspic*, the 1970 *Myra Breckinridge* and, from the same year, *Cotton Comes to Harlem*.

In 1974, the same year in which he starred in the horror film *The Beast Must Die*, he was appointed actor-in-residence at the Royal Shakespeare Company, Stratford-upon-Avon while, before his death in 2007, he also guest starred in a number of episodes of the television soap *Dynasty*.

From the stage to the circus big top, **George William Lockhart** and his brother **Samuel Lockhart** were celebrated elephant trainers – while one of them was to die in tragic circumstances.

Born respectively in 1849 and 1851, they were the sons of the English-born **Sam Lockhart**, a stilt-walking clown, and Hannah Pinder of the French circus family of Pinder.

The brothers toured widely with their parents, performing as clowns, acrobats and bareback riders until, in the early 1870s, George bought his first elephant, Boney, followed by Molly and Waddy, whom the brothers trained in acts including one riding a tricycle.

Touring the British music hall scene, performing before Queen Victoria, and also much further abroad, throughout 1895 they are reputed to have performed 500 times at Proctor's Pleasure Palace, in New York.

The next troupe of elephants – Salt, Pepper, Sauce and Mustard and known as 'The Cruet' – also proved highly popular, with Sauce and Mustard being replaced after they died by Vinegar and Baby.

But tragedy struck in 1904 when George Lockhart was crushed to death when the elephants stampeded while being led through a railway goods yard in Walthamstow, London.

His brother Samuel, meanwhile, who had also worked for a time in the United States for the Ringling Brothers Circus and continued to tour throughout the UK with his elephant act, features in a number of books on the history of circus and is also the central character in Janet Storrie's children's book *Elephants at Royal Leamington Spa*, published in 1990.

He died in 1933, the uncle of his brother's son **George Claude Lockhart**.

Born in 1885 and keeping up the family circus tradition, he was the ringmaster for a number of years at Blackpool Tower Circus and the International Circus at Belle Vue, Manchester.

Having worked at Blackpool up until 1945 and also recognised as the first ringmaster to adopt what became the 'trademark' attire of black top hat, white shirt and gloves and pink huntsman's tails, he died in 1979 – while eight years later Lockhart Close, on the former site of Belle Vue Zoo, was named in his honour.

In the highly competitive world of sport, **Jackie Lockhart**, born in 1965 in Stonehaven, Kincardine and Mearns, is the Scottish curler who has played for her nation at Olympic level; winner of a bronze medal at the 2007 World Women's Curling Championship, she comments on the game for television.

Still on the ice, **Thomas Lockhart** was the American ice hockey administrator, events promoter and business manager who in 1937 became founding president of the Amateur Hockey Association – later US Hockey; business manager of the New York Rangers and an inductee of the United States Hockey Hall of Fame, he died in 1979.

On the race track, **Frank Lockhart**, born in 1903 in Dayton, Ohio, was the American automobile racing driver and custom car constructor whose many triumphs include winning the 1926 Indianapolis 500.

An inductee of the Motorsports Hall of Fame and the National Sprint Car Hall of Fame, he was killed at Daytona Beach in 1928 when attempting to set a new land speed record.

In the rather less dangerous sport of Irish

Gaelic football, **Seán Lockhart** is the champion player born in 1976 in Banagher, Northern Ireland.

Winner of three National League titles, an Ulster Senior Football Championship and also a talented hurler, he holds the record for the highest number of appearances – between 1998 and 2006 – for Ireland in the International Rules Series.

Bearers of the Lockhart name have also excelled in the creative world of music.

Born in Edinburgh in 1930, **James Lockhart** is the distinguished Scottish conductor, pianist and organist whose posts have included music director, from 1968 to 1972, at Welsh National Opera, the Staatstheater Kassel in Germany from 1972 to 1978 and, from 1986 to 1992, director of the Royal College of Music, London – where he originally studied.

Born in 1959 in Poughkeepsie, New York, **Keith Lockhart** is the American conductor who has held posts including conductor of the Boston Pops Orchestra, principal conductor of the BBC Concert Orchestra and, later, chief guest conductor of the orchestra.

In the equally creative world of art, **William Ewart Lockhart** was the Scottish Victorian painter of noted works including *The Jubilee Celebration in*

Westminster Abbey, June 21, 1887, commissioned by Queen Victoria and now part of the Royal Collection.

Born in 1846 in Eaglesfield, Dumfriesshire, a member of the Royal Scottish Academy and an associate of the Royal Watercolour Society, he died in 1900.

A Scottish watercolour painter whose subjects were decidedly less grand than Queen Victoria, **William Mustart Lockhart** was born in Perth in 1885 – Perth Prison to be exact, where his father was a warder and on whose grounds his parents lived.

Apprenticed as an upholsterer he later moved to Glasgow, settling in the east end of the city and establishing a picture restoration, upholstery and furniture manufacturing business.

But art was his abiding passion and, after studying under the artist Thomas Fairbairn, he became noted for his work featuring Glasgow's east end, particularly the Bridgeton area; he died in 1941.

From art to literature, **John Gibson Lockhart** was the Scottish literary critic and author born in 1794 in the manse of Cambusnethan House, Lanarkshire.

A critic for Edinburgh's famed *Blackwood's Magazine*, it was through his friendship with Sir

Walter Scott that he met and married the great antiquarian and novelist's eldest daughter, Sophia.

A gifted author in his own right, he is best known for the definitive biography of his father-in-law, *Life of Sir Walter Scott*, published in seven volumes between 1837 and 1838 and a second edition, expanded to ten volumes, published in 1839.

The subject of a painting by the artist Robert Scott Lauder, who executed a number of works based on Scott's novels, he died in 1854 and is buried in Dryburgh Abbey, in the Borders, close to Sir Walter's grave.